15 Poems to Healing & Recovery is a wonderful l[...] women who have long histories of drug addicti[...] early age. They can identify with your beautiful and som[...] poetry that will help them bring out their feelings. Thank you for producing such a thought provoking and helpful document.

> David H. Kerr
> Founding President and CEO (1968 - 2010), Integrity House
> Newark, New Jersey

In effect, Dr. Kaufman has forged a new model of writing poetry, a poetry that works more generously for the reader and serves as a healing tool... the poetry has a universal appeal... As a heartfelt contribution to the world of creative arts therapies, Dr. Kaufman has created a series of poems in a workbook format, which will stir the hearts and minds of patients and therapists in many worlds.

> Karen D. Goodman, MS, RMT, LCAT
> Professor, Music Therapy
> Montclair State University

A compelling read for anyone who desires to heal, grow, or find their place in the world. Doctor Kaufman bares her soul in an effort to help others to connect the dots, and make sense of the stops, in their own journey. The prescription may be intended as "poetic medicine" for professionals to use in their practice with adults and teens but I recommend it for anyone searching to find their authentic self. The book is sure to advance the field of poetry therapy and promote discourse among creative arts therapists.

> Karen D. Carbonello, MA
> Executive Director, SAFE
> Hunterdon, Flemington, New Jersey

What an in-depth, layered yet also accessible container for people healing, for people in recovery! Reading this book by Dr. Diane Kaufman, I am at first deeply impressed with an expertise informed by a compassionate thoughtfulness. Dr. Kaufman knows what she is doing here but she is sharing this because of how much she truly cares. What I am saying is this: poet-psychiatrist-woman-human being forms a creative, integral whole and that has become this useful and beautiful offering. Beyond this, the final word belongs to the capacity of *15 Poems to Healing & Recovery* to EMPOWER and HONOR any person willing to begin.

> John Fox, BA, CPT
> The Institute for Poetic Medicine

15 Poems
to Healing & Recovery

by Diane Kaufman, MD

contents

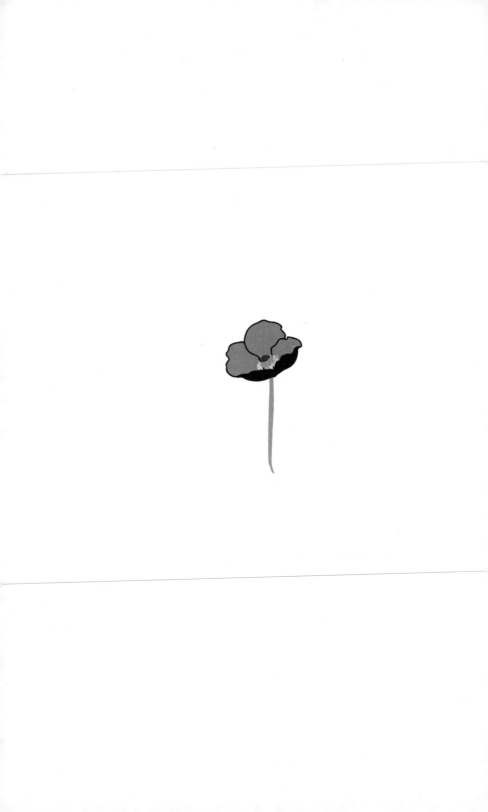

Forward to the First Edition

When I first read Dr. Diane Kaufman's manuscript, which is now this astounding work of poetry and healing, what struck me most, was that her words were a rich and gentle invitation. As I read each poem and each of the accompanying questions, I sat with wonder. I sat with swelling gratitude. I thought about the individuals who would read *Cracking Up and Back Again: Transformation Through Poetry* the healers and those seeking wholeness, and I was imbued with the knowledge that this book would offer so very much. That this book had to be on bookshelves, in hands. That it had to be birthed.

The title itself is sheer affirmation and speaks to: hope and possibility. The phrase 'cracking up' has most often been seen in a negative light. What *Cracking Up and Back Again: Transformation Through Poetry* honors, is that without the cracks, the light has no space in which to enter. And light, of course, gives us a way to navigate the darkness. Dr. Kaufman's brilliant work shows that in trusting not only will the light shine through the cracks, but also that transformation will come.

Important, relevant, and challenging questions follow each moving and insightful poem and pave a beckoning road upon which healer and seeker can venture with the full knowledge that their journey together towards wholeness, will be realized, in their time, with trust and guidance.

What is most vital with *Cracking Up and Back Again: Transformation Through Poetry* is its honesty. In order for any individual to enter into the work of healing, it is required that the soul is laid bare. It is a must that silences are broken, that the reflection that stares back at us from the mirror is ours. Is acknowledged. Is owned.

Dr. Diane Kaufman's spirit, which pulsates through her words, invites you to trust that you will find transformation. That even with your sorrow and grief, your words will come, and that the light will shine through the cracks. And that you will embrace its glow.

Margot Van Sluytman
Publisher, Palabras Press
2007

Introduction

Poetry Speaks
Poetry is silence before words
Poetry is born from the unspoken
Poetry is breathe in, pause, exhale
Poetry is one voice expressing to be heard
Poetry created and creates the world
Poetry speaks and says all

As a physician and poet, I believe that psychiatry is in danger of limiting understanding of being human to a sum total of chemical parts, when its exclusive focus is on the body. Poetry illuminate the deeper human being. Poets, since the beginning of time, have expressed and recorded the yearning of the human spirit. Poets are fellow travelers, and poetry is life's consciousness captured on paper, still wanting and able to be seen, heard, and felt. Poetry can help guide us through life's terror and wonders, as we, too, contemplate our place in this world. As we journey into poetry, we are invited, welcomed, and urged to reclaim our poetic voice, to speak our truth, and be heard as valuable members of the all too human family. Poetry deepens understanding of self and other, encouraging growth and transformation. It is a powerful prescription in the healing of traumatized children and adults. Through poetry we directly experience the art and mind of emotional healing.

Please know that I am not prescribing poetry as a substitute for mental health treatment, and I encourage you to seek all the professional help, guidance, and support that you may need. What I am suggesting is that reading and writing poetry, for some, can be a rescuing life line, an invisible yet real refuge, where one finds safe haven and friends, who speak and listen, and want what is best for you. This has been my experience of poetry.

The poetry of *15 Poems to Healing & Recovery* (previously titled *Cracking Up and Back Again: Transformation Through Poetry)* were inspired by my own life experiences. In writing them, I came to know myself better, and was helped to "write" myself into a greater appreciation and understanding of life and living. The poems were put together as a workbook for residents of Integrity House, a residential drug treatment program in Newark, New Jersey. I felt the poems were universal, and as such, could serve as writing prompts and as invitations to look within. This "essence" is what the group members and I experienced.

I see this poetry collection as being of use to women and men confronting and opening up to themselves when they are experiencing dark nights and lost days. As such, residents of substance abuse programs, prisons, and shelters may benefit. For those who have had difficult life experiences such as sexual abuse and adult violence, the poetry may serve as a witness and supportive guide towards hoped for recovery. Mental health professionals in reading these poems may gain insight into the inner world of the abused child grown into adulthood who has wrestled with demons, survived, and thrived, willing and able to express the pain of self and others, and the joy of new growth and transformation. It is hoped that the reader of these poems will gain a personal understanding of how poetry can be of help in healing the wounded self, and of poetry being a bountiful resource that can be utilized in therapeutic treatment.

Individuals wanting to know more about the healing powers of poetry are directed to the resources at the end of the book. For now, let me just say that poetry therapy goes back to ancient times, to the Oracle of Delphi, to the God of Poetry, Apollo, who was also the God of Medicine.

If in any way these poems are too direct and too painful, evoking memories too difficult to surmount, please put the book aside. Listen well to your inner voice that yearns to advise and comfort you. Perhaps this is not the book for you, or it is not the right time. If you are in therapy, please share with your therapist your thoughts, feelings, and memories when reading these poems. Always remember, you are not alone. For those of you who are able to safely journey to poetry and enter the sometimes dark, but always luminous inner world, I welcome you, and reach out my hand. I wish you strength, hope, and blessings on your recovery journey.

In kinship,
Diane Kaufman, MD

1. Poetic Medicine

There's always a big black pot
Simmering
Bubbling
Boiling over with troubles
Scalded air rising hot
Burning eyes and skin
A big wooden spoon
Hands spellbound
Can't release the grip
Stirring wildly
Stirring non-stopping
And it's always darkest night
The brew gets thicker and thicker
As more troubles keep piling in
You ask yourself, "Oh! When will it ever end?"
A whisper replies, "Pour out the pot and start all over again!"

The "pot" which is our own vessel of being will surely break as in "breakdown or crackpot" unless we do something about "it" and ourselves. The poetry you are about to read is one person's perilous journey to become and be real. It is by surrendering ourselves to the process of learning through life, that life as our teacher, reveals to us the essence of what it means to be alive. When one person breaks silence, the truth in all of us gains strength. There comes a time when the only answer that makes sense is to, "pour out the pot and begin all over again." When we empty ourselves of our false nature, we are ready to be filled by a power greater than ourselves, which is Nature, itself. Are you ready to take your "poetic medicine?" How sick do you have to make yourself in order to get well?

2. Cracking Up

I'm cracking up
Piece by piece
Part by part
Moment by moment
I wish I could just dissolve
But that's not the way it goes

Have you ever felt like you were losing your mind or you had lost your mind? What did it feel like? Why was is happening? How long did it last? Did you ever get your mind back again? What did you learn?

3. Who I Am

I can't show you who I am
I'm ugly
I'm worthless
I'm nothing
You can't love who I am
No one can love who I am
No one has ever loved who I am
I will have to kill myself
Because being dead will be the
Only way I can hide once more

Sometimes we can really hate who we are or feel hatred for what we have done. We are out of balance and lose all sense of compassion. We forget the "good" and magnify and think only about the "bad." We lose out "wholeness." We imagine ourselves as unlovable and incapable of loving. Have you ever felt like that? What was going on outside (in your life) and inside (within your head) when it happened? Where are those feelings now?

4. I Am So Sorry

I am so sorry that I can't be
Who you want me to be
I can't help the way I am
Don't you know how painful
It is to be me
If I could change I would
How I would obliterate this me
I am shackled by
I can't help it
You don't understand
You never understand
You want me to be different
I can't do it
It's too much for me to do
I don't have the strength
I am so ashamed of myself
Why can't I be someone else
I don't want to be me anymore
I just want to go to sleep
I want to have a beautiful dream
And never wake up

When we do not know who we are, we may start to live our lives for other people. We try to be only who they want us to be. In so doing, we neglect and forget our own true inner self. Because we can never become who we are not, this way of non-being called co-dependency, is extremely painful. Have you ever experienced these feelings?

5. Questions to a Child

Were you abused?
Were you abused?
I was
I was
Do feel the silent shame?
I do
I do
Do you waken in the night
Tears across your face
Crying and enraged?
I do
Can you not forget it happened
And still wonder if it did?
I do
Do your wrists pulsate in pain
Asking you to cut them
With memories that haunt you
And still won't go away?
Mine do
Do you doubt who you are
And wished it never happened
And ask yourself
Over and over again
Why didn't I shout louder
Why didn't someone listen
Am I to blame?
I do
Do you see the children suffer
And want to see that pain
To feel their reality
And live their life again?
I do
Do you make the chance
To shout aloud
Stop! Listen!
A child is hurting
Do something now!
I do
Does your voice become a whisper
From crying out
So loud and long

Waiting for them to see
Waiting for them to do
What must be done?
Mine does
Do you ask your God for strength
To shout until they hear you?
I do
Dear child
Were you abused?
Were you abused?
I was
I was

There are many men and women who have had abuse experiences. As children, we may have witnessed violence between our parents. We may have been physically beaten, sexually abused, and emotionally damaged. Even as adults, the abuse may have continued as we experienced rape or domestic violence with "love" partners or strangers. Some of us may have behaved abusively ourselves, as we grew older but not wiser. Has the violence known as abuse touched your life? How healed are you from these experiences? What do you need from yourself and other to get and stay well?

6. What is Love

He loves me
He loves me not
What is love
What is love not
How do I feel it
How do I give it
How much is it
Does it cost too much
Everyone says I want to be in love
It's every love song's lyric
It's every heartbreak's sweet lament
Captive of love
You've got me under your spell
Wishing on a star
You are my belle
What the hell is love
Do I even want it
Do I want to give it
Maybe it belongs to you instead
No thank you I'm on a love free diet
Try me next week when I can't control my appetite
Does love make the world go 'round
Does it make my heart go pitter patter
Or just make me love sick to my stomach
How much love is enough
Will too much clog my arteries
Heart attack and heart break
Two for the price of one
I must remember
I must never forget
One fine day
I'll wake up dead
Too late then for regrets
Do you think I'm taking it all too seriously
Excuse me but...
What do you think of love
Have you found the answer yet
Or know what love's not
Won't you tell me love's secret
Pretty please
With sugar on top

We all have our story. Once upon a time a child was born. The chapters in our lives are all about love. For some, it's a comedy and they may play the fool. Others write a tragedy and their part is the suffering martyr. Others write an epic adventure of hero and heroine who search for "true love" by slaying the dragon, scaling the mountain, and conquering the most fearsome foe of all: their very own false heart. Do you ever wonder about love? What kind of love story have you written? What kind of love story do you want to write? What kind of love story are you writing right now? How can you enhance the quality of love in your life?

7. Now I Know

Now I know
It was because I saw your heart
You were wide open
And I looked inside
There it was
A red sparkling jewel
It was beating
It was weeping
It was bursting with love
To share
And feel
And I know
You must have seen
And known
That inside me
There is a heart
Too
Now I know

We all want to love and be loved. Life might have hardened our skins and even hardened our hearts, but true love is what we still desire. Often we think it is someone else loving us that will release us. That may be so, but the deepest, most powerful love is the love within our very own heart. Whatever you choose to call it: soul, spirit, higher power, or God within, it is this inner love that sets us free and gives welcome and freedom to all we meet. How open or closed is your heart? What made it so? What kind of heart do you want to have?

8. How It Feels

I am a flame on fire
Being with you I am
Electric currents shooting
Across the body
Electrification inside and out
Rising from the essential core
Reaching all extremities
Simultaneously in pulsing ecstasy
I can feel it through
My fingertip releasing
As my hand touches yours

Sexual attraction and love are a powerful combination and can create good and bad explosions in our lives. What have been the most intense love relationships in your life? What did you learn from these experiences? Do you have any advice to give a friend who can't see straight because of "too hot" love and sex?

9. The Hole in My Heart

There's a hole in my heart
I kept forgetting where it was
I thought it was between my legs
I wanted you there to fill me up

There's a hole in my heart
I kept forgetting where it was
I thought it was in my mind
I begged God please fill me up

There's a hole in my heart
I kept forgetting where it was
I thought it was my eyes
I prayed for visions to take
The black away

There's a hole in my heart
I kept forgetting where it was
I thought it was missing you
And all I could do was cry

There's a hole in my heart
I kept forgetting where it was
Sometimes feeling it grow larger
It swallows me up

There's a hole in my heart
I kept forgetting where it was
A hole in this heart
A hole in my heart
A hole in a heart

There's a...

Sometimes we run away from our own pain into the arms of another because we want them to fill all the "holes" in us. When they don't, because they can't, we get angry or sad or run off with another lover. What holes are you trying to fill up through love, sex, drugs, and other addictions? Where did your emptiness come from and what needs to happen so you can feel you "wholeness" again?

10. The Place of Forgiveness

If I could reach this hand
And touch that place called forgiveness
How I would stretch these fingers
These muscle sinews wrapped around dry bone
To reach
To grasp
To finally know
A fingertip absolved of pain
Five-fingered hand released of suffering
The wrist at peace at last
Traveling up the arm
Skin shivered hair on end
These shoulders would bend
To hollowed chambers of a heart
Cascading in a sea of blood
Here just beneath the skin
That never protected me
Is the place of forgiveness
Where tears wash clean
If I could but reach this hand
And touch that sacred place
I would that I could
I must know that I can

"To err is human and to forgive divine," was said by a famous someone long ago. Guilt for wrong-doings can be a heavy burden. Anger and vengeance towards those who hurt us is a heavy weight, too. Feeling like a victim can be equally oppressive. Forgiveness can help. For what do you seek forgiveness and from whom? Do you need to forgive another? Do you need to forgive yourself? Can you remember anyone ever forgiving you for something you said or did? Do you have any spiritual beliefs on forgiveness? How do they help you? Do you believe forgiveness is necessary or not?

11. I Am This

I am this
I am more than this
I am not experience alone
I exist beyond the moment
I am ephemeral
I am change
I am choice
I am alive within this body
Chosen just for me
Given the chance
How do I choose to live my life
May there be but one word: yes!
Coming from my mouth
Flowing from my heart
Out to the welcoming world
Then back again through breath
Willingly inspired
Deeply inhaled
Inside
To the place where truth resides
Divinity Rapture Love
I am this
I am much more than this
I am

Our spiritual self is always alive even when we come to doubt its very existence. We can make the choice to be spiritually reborn and live a life full of meaning, joy, and creative purpose. We can learn from our mistakes along the way and become a guide to those who need our help, and believe me, we are all in need of help and loving kindness. Do you believe that you have a "spiritual" self? If so, how does your "spirit" express itself? What kind of human being do you want to be in this life of yours? Do you think there is a purpose to your being here? What is it? If you see no purpose to your life, how do you plan to use your time here on earth?

12. Secret Ambition

I have a secret ambition
In this heart
To stand up and strut my stuff
To dance like wild
Green eyes on fire
In high high heels
And ruby lips
Holding you at finger tips
There's a secret ambition
In this heart
I just can't escape
Beneath the calm
That takes me every place
Could it be that
It's not too late
To be myself
And tell it all
Be brave at last
Forget the past
And come alive
I have a secret ambition
That fills me up
That calls the shots
Won't let me rest
Till truth be told
Of what I'm going through
Could it be so easy now
To come to this
After years of hiding
From myself
Cause no one else
Believed in me
Not even myself
I have a secret ambition
It's calling me now
A future at my fingertips
No more to wait
Don't hesitate
To live the secret ambition
Right now
The secret ambition in this heart

Is freedom from what I used to be
It won't stop calling me
Till I am who I am meant to be
There is a secret ambition in this heart
That guides me
Wants what's best for me
And won't stop calling me
Till I'm free I'm free
There is a secret ambition in this heart
It's the destination where I'm going
And I'm growing ever closer
Whenever it calls
Out my name
To me

Do you have a secret ambition that's locked away in your heart? What's stopping you from fulfilling that dream? Your creative positive energy is meant to come out, but only you can release it! How can you free up that energy? And are you willing to begin right now? If not, ask yourself why.

13. A Strange Feeling

It is a strange feeling
That I am having
I feel like I am
About to shed my skin
And step outside
Whole
I am the one
Inside and waiting
Wanting to crawl out
Through the eyes
Through the hands
Out through the mouth
It is going to happen
Soon
I can feel it
Inside
Where I am still being
Skin will be discarded
It will be my foot
Seen kicking it away
It is a strange feeling
That I am having

We think we are an "adult" or a "grown-up" just because we get older. That's not true at all. Isn't it about time to stop lying and finally tell the truth? Time and age may give us the experiences, but only we can transform our painful experiences into knowledge and right action. And we can do that if we want to hard enough and long enough and deep enough and with the right spirit, which is one of humility. Pride and anger never get us anywhere, and the sooner we learn that lesson, the better. In nature it happens all the time. The beautiful butterfly grows from the caterpillar. The tadpole gives way to the frog. And we can emerge as truly humane human beings if we choose to choose over and over again to grow and learn and be the best we can be, just because this is what our hearts tell us that our lives are meant to be. How are you transforming yourself? Who do you want to be and become? How close are you to achieving your goals? Will you make it?

14. The Power of One

Can one person save the world
Can one person help the world
Can one person be in the world
One alone
Many together
To love and care
It starts with one
Be the one who loves
Be the one who cares
Be the one who makes the difference
One person can change the world

You might be thinking, "Well, I'm just one person, so what on earth difference does it make what I do with my life?" It makes all the difference in the world! You are meant to be here and that's why you were born. Please don't waste your life away. Please don't throw your life away. Your spirit is part of all of life's spirit and we need you! No one else on earth has your special gifts, and no one else on earth ever will again. It's a once in a lifetime opportunity, and the buyer needn't beware. So, what will your "difference" be? Can you make that difference today? Will you do it? Pray that you do because in so doing, you will be transforming yourself most beautifully, for it is in "giving that we shall receive."

15. Yesterday My Heart Cracked Open

Yesterday
My heart cracked open
All birds in the sky
Flew within

Yesterday
My heart cracked open
There was thunder
Lightening
Downpour rain
My thirsty earth drank it
Flowers again

Yesterday
My heart cracked open
There were you and I
There was nothing
Different between us
We were just
The same

Yesterday
My heart cracked open
There was I
There was nothing
That was not different
I will never
Be the same

Friend
I pray for you
Your heart to crack
Wide open
Be not afraid
Be free instead

Yesterday
My heart cracked open
All birds in the sky
Flew within
And I like they
Have wings

Cracking open to our Higher Power and the creative energy within is our spiritual and transformative rebirth. Our earthly task is to transform pain (and joy) into understanding, and despair (and elation) into inspiration. It can be done if this is the path we choose not just once, but each and every day of our life. God bestows blessings upon us all. May we in turn bless ourselves by becoming true to our higher nature. We are all beautiful flowers. Isn't it time we blossomed in the garden?

May God bless you and keep you from harm. And may peace find a home within you.

Afterword

These words "after" are dedicated to the power of self-realization within us all.

How to Define the Poet

A voice
A message
A need to express
A need to be heard
A need that goes beyond mere words
A practiced gift in choosing words, shaping phrases,
and delivering "sound" messages that travel through space
and time

Finding One's Voice

Is not easy
But is the essential requirement
All else is futile as imitation is a fraud
We must begin to know ourselves from the inside out
There is no substitute for being one's self
Life's hardest task
And greatest joy

And What If We...

Forgot
Misplaced
Neglected
Put aside
Never practiced
Discarded
Our own true voice

Not to worry...

A poet has been there before you
Leaving words on paper behind
Experience is the poem
Are you listening as you read?
Can you hear the poet's voice?
This poem was written for you

Poetry Resources

I am especially inspired by the writings of Rumi, Emily Dickinson, Sharon Olds, Mary Oliver, and William Stafford to name just a few. Do not hesitate to find the poets who will speak the words that you need to hear. They are waiting patiently, and they yearn to be taken in by you. They will be the best of company on your life's journey.

There are countless books and online resources for poetry. Please got to your library, bookstore, and computer as soon as possible to claim your wealth in the life experiences and life lessons described by individual poets and collected within poetry anthologies, guides to the craft of writing, and resources on poetry therapy. Some of the many worthwhile poetry therapy websites to discover include The National Association for Poetry Therapy, The Creative "Righting" Center, and the Institute for Poetic Medicine.

Below are some books on creativity, writing and poetry that have spoken to me. These and many more, may speak to you.

Butterworth, Eric. *The Creative Life: 7 Keys to Your Inner Genius*. New York: Jeremy P. Tarcher/Putnam, 2003.

Cameron, Julia. *The Right to Write: An Invitation and Initiation into the Writing Life*. New York: Jeremy P. Tarcher/ Putnam, 1998.

Fox, John. *Poetic Medicine*. New York: Jeremy P. Tarcher/ Putnam, 1997.

Jerome, Judson. *The Poet and the Poem: The Comprehensive Guide to Writing and Assessing Poetry*. Cincinnati, Ohio: Writer's Digest Books, 1974.

Leedy, Jack J. (editor) *Poetry as Healer Mending the Troubled Mind*. New York: The Vanguard Press, 1985.

May, Rollo. *The Courage to Create*. New York: WW Norton and Company, 1975.

Oliver, Mary. *A Poetry Handbook*. New York: Harcourt, Inc., 1994.

Peacock, Molly. *How to Read a Poem...and Start a Poetry Circle*. New York: Riverhead Books, 1999.

Pennebaker, James W. *Writing to Heal: A Guided Journal for Recovering from Trauma and Emotional Upheaval*. Oakland, California: New Harbinger Publications, 2004.

About the Author

Dr. Diane Kaufman is a poet and artist. She is also a child psychiatrist with more than thirty years of clinical experience, first in Newark, New Jersey, and now in Portland, Oregon. She was honored in 2000 and 2011 for her practice of humanism in medicine by the Healthcare Foundation of New Jersey. Dr. Kaufman's passion and gift is transforming trauma into creativity. She is the author of the healing from trauma story, *Bird That Wants to Fly,* which inspired a children's opera composed by Michael Raphael, performed by Trilogy: An Opera Company, and narrated by the actor, Danny Glover.

Dr. Kaufman presents internationally on arts and healing. She was the keynote speaker at the 2016 National Association for Poetry Therapy Conference. Dr. Kaufman is available for workshops, training and consultation. For more information about Dr. Kaufman, her published works, and the healing value of creativity, please the website, www.artsmedicineforhealthandhealing.com.

15 Poems to Healing & Recovery
Arts Medicine Transformation Curriculum

by Diane Kaufman, MD

Introduction

The *15 Poems to Healing & Recovery* text is a poetic journey from despair to recovery. The poems have universal themes that encourage reflection and shared discussion. In experiencing the poetry and its accompanying prose prompts, it is hoped that a parallel process towards recovery will be evoked and inspired in the reader's own consciousness. The use of the book has been expanded in the Arts Medicine Transformation Curriculum to include many forms of expressive arts creation rather than just poetry alone.

The purpose of the Arts Medicine Transformation Curriculum is to apply expressive arts healing modalities to the repertoire of addiction recovery treatments. The curriculum was developed as a therapeutic companion to *15 Poems to Healing & Recovery* (previously titled *Cracking Up and Back Again: Transformation Through Poetry*). The curriculum was originally written as the final project for Dr. Kaufman's Expressive Arts Educational Facilitation certification from Salve Regina University's Expressive Arts Institute Program. In the spirit of collaboration, it is now offered to addiction treatment agencies and workshop leaders as a healing resource. The curriculum is meant to inspire your own creativity and may be a starting point in developing expressive arts workshops for *15 Poems to Healing & Recovery* or expressive arts workshops for other inspired writings. Use the curriculum as a guide and use it as is, or it may be modified, expanded and grown to best meet the unique needs of the women and men in recovery whom you serve.

As detailed in *Art and Healing: Using Expressive Art to Heal Your Body, Mind, and Spirit* by Barbara Ganim, expressive art is process not product oriented, and uses the body-mind's language of imagery to expand our ability to heal far beyond where words alone can take us. Making imagistic expressive art coupled with the conscious intention to heal, taps into the strength of our intuitive and creative right brain.

Verbalizing what we find there is a function of the rational and linear left brain. The contrast and interplay between thought (cognition) and feeling (emotion) is integrated as we are guided to truly "feel our feelings" centered in the body, rather than to just "think about our feelings" in our head. Combining both the right brain and left brain abilities through expressive art can lead to deeper awareness, appreciation, and acceptance of our inner experience. Growing positively from this inner experience is further facilitated through Barbara Ganim's stated process of "ART: Access, Release, and Transform." First the stressful inner experience is given form within the body-mind as an image. Next this image is released externally as forms of art. Finally, the negative feelings and emotions evoke transformation into new and empowering healing images as we communicate with ourselves through the language of art which is metaphor. Expressive art accesses the inner co-creative artist within us all. It is an overflowing inner resource which inspires us towards our highest good. For men and women in recovery, workshops including expressive art modalities can provide an experience of non-judgmental self-awareness within the context of a supportive group environment. ART (access, release, and transform) promotes personal responsibility by choosing constructive images to cope with stress, and helps to strengthen and heal the wounded self. These images are made real in the form of art to be danced, sung, drawn, and/or written. Knowing that we are all born with the potential to express our own unique creativity is very powerful. It is through creativity that a destructive past can be changed into a life-affirming present and future. To internalize this knowledge, however, our creativity must be directly experienced. Expressive art is a healing process towards this end.

Please be aware, however, that no matter how valuable the Arts Medicine Transformation Curriculum may be for participating group members, it is not meant to replace mental health treatment or a referral for psychological or psychiatric evaluation services. These healing workshops are meant to be an added resource to support addiction recovery and sustained sobriety.

The powerful spoken word performance, "Desperate Love," available on the Arts Medicine for Health and Healing website (www.artsmedicineforhealthandhealing.com)

within the Healing Connections section, will be utilized in the workshop series. It can also be shown to individuals not participating in the full curriculum to promote their reflection on addiction and recovery, the highs and lows and the ultimate price to be paid. The poem easily lends itself to self-inquiry writing responses based upon the dramatized lines of the poem and the story it tells, beginning with its opening question, "What's your desperate love?"

Implementation

The Arts Medicine Transformation Curriculum is designed to be implemented at addiction recovery intensive outpatient and/or residential treatment programs. It is envisioned as starting with a "train the trainer" model with continuing education credits provided to staff if this can be arranged. Within the therapeutic community setting, these staff counselors actively engage, challenge, and support individuals on their continued recovery journey. Many of these counselors are also in recovery. Through their own struggles with drugs and alcohol leading to hard won sobriety, they have much to offer their clients. Now, with these participating counselors having direct experience of the transformative healing power of the expressive arts, they will be both inspired and prepared to facilitate the Arts Medicine Transformation Curriculum with women and men at their own particular agency.

The expressive arts curriculum program is held on site at the specific organization. The group meets weekly for twelve weeks for two hours per week. If the staff is unable to arrange this schedule, a change in meeting length and frequency, as well as weekend intensive trainings could be considered. The ideal group size is ten to twelve participants upwards to fifteen participants, but up to twenty participants could be allowed, depending on the facilitator's expertise. A co-facilitator would be beneficial in larger group settings. Each participant is given a copy of *15 Poems to Healing & Recovery*. The facilitator (and organization) will provide the art materials and supplies for each session. There should be healthy snacks and beverages available for refreshment. If participants are unable to attend a session, they are expected to call or email the facilitator regarding their absence. If the facilitator has an emergency and is unavailable for the session, she/he needs to be in touch with the sponsoring organization, such that another facilitator can be identified who will lead the workshop, or if necessary, the workshop will be canceled and rescheduled. There are no exclusionary criteria for participating in the workshop series other than active addiction, or stated resistance to enrolling in the program. Participation is voluntary, but once enrolled, participants are expected to attend all sessions, to actively participate, and to behave in a respectful manner.

Participants will be reassured that one does not need to be a trained or gifted artist to benefit from the group experience. What is required is the willingness to go inside and get in touch with inner feelings, thoughts and images which can be released and further transformed. The participants will also be reassured that the group is confidential, non-competitive and non-judgmental. Each person within the group will have his or her own unique and valuable experience. The facilitator will be available to meet with group members on an individual basis as warranted. If referral for mental health treatment is indicated, the facilitator will convey this need to appropriate staff within the organization. Group members will be encouraged to keep an Arts Medicine Healing Journal in words and images to help them reflect upon their experiences in the expressive arts program.

Expressive Arts Workshops

During the Arts Medicine Transformation Curriculum workshop series, the poetry and writing prompts from *15 Poems to Healing & Recovery* will be shared and discussed. Further ideas on how to integrate expressive arts into the group experience are outlined in the workshop sessions below. The "train the trainer" group staff members are required to read *Art and Healing: Using Expressive Art to Heal Your Body, Mind, and Spirit* by Barbara Ganim as a prerequisite to joining the workshop series. Included in that text are the series of questions to be used in dialogue with images which will be drawn during the sessions. The "train the trainer" participants who go on the become facilitators, will need to have experience in addiction recovery counseling, group facilitation, and also be open to active engagement in creative expression for healing purposes.

Session One

The goal of session one is for participants to gain understanding of what expressive art is, and how expressive arts help heal. Within this context, the group will also begin to bond with each other as fellow travelers on a shared journey towards healing. The music video *I'm Here* on the tragic deaths of Bobbi Kristina Brown and Whitney Houston will be shown as an example of expressive art for addiction recovery as the song is based upon the poem, "To All Hearts That Break," written by Diane Kaufman, MD. The video is available in the Poetry Baby Blog section of the Arts Medicine for Health and Healing website. Group members will discuss their reactions to the song and video. The song is meant to inspire the need for recovery and the need for creative and innovative approaches to recovery, as death, unfortunately, can be the final outcome for men and women still trapped inside their addiction.

The different qualities of left brain function versus right brain function will be reviewed as an invitation to "take a walk on the right (creative) side." The stress response and ART process should be discussed and reviewed as detailed in Barbara Ganim's book, *Art and Healing: Using Expressive Art to Heal Your Body, Mind, and Spirit.* The use of expressive arts as a modality helpful in supporting addiction recovery will be suggested as a strategy (and an enjoyable one) to be used in one's "creative recovery tool box." The group members will also be asked to share their own experience with the creative arts. The poem "Cracking Open" will be shared with the group members:

Cracking Up
Cracking Down
Sideways Always
Through & Between
Cracking Forward
Cracking Backward
Within & Against
Cracking Wide
Cracking Open
United & Apart
Together & Forever
Cracking Then

Cracking Now
Spirit Within
Seeds of My Life
Yearning Am I
To Be & To Live
Cracking Free

There will be a guided meditation to go "inside" and to see and feel if there is something within that wants to grow, to crack free, has cracked free, or is unable to crack free. If the group member is not able to sense this, then she/he will be asked to focus on the feeling that accompanies the need for cracking open. The group members will be asked to draw this feeling, image, thought, or sensation. Upon completion they will be asked to write responses to what they have drawn. Following this, another image will be drawn based upon an inner felt sense of what else is needed to further the cracking open and healing process. The members will discuss their ART experience with a partner. The session will end with everyone in a circle, being led in a guided meditation to imagine the creative healing source within, as they listen to the resonating sound of a Tibetan singing bowl or other musical accompaniment.

Session Two

The goal of session two is to introduce participants to the *15 Poems to Healing & Recovery* book and its further expansion into the expressive arts. The session will begin with a brief review of session one. Members will share what they took with them from that experience. Next each member will be given a copy of the poetry book to keep. The first poem, "Poetic Medicine," will be read aloud by several of the group members so that it can be heard in different voices. The writing prompt is also read aloud. This will lead into discussion of the poem's possible meanings, especially from the vantage point of addiction and recovery. How the poem relates to the 12 Steps of Alcoholics Anonymous will be discussed. How does a person who is in the throes of addiction respond to "more troubles piling in" versus a person who is in recovery? How do we "start all over again?" How do we reshape ourselves? Next, after a meditation to listen in silence to the "healing voice" within, the group will be asked to write a poem or prose piece in response to what was shared in the discussion. The energy of these writings will next be expressed as a drawing. These drawings can be discussed in the group. The session will end with a ritual closing of the members standing in a circle and expressing aloud a healing word with an accompanying physical movement that embodies that word to be shared with the group and with the intention to release it safely into the center of the circle where it will be contained, as new ingredients for their inner healing vessel. The facilitator will need to keep track of the words that were spoken. When all members have had their turn, they go around again and may take from the center of the circle a healing word and its physical movement that had been expressed by another that they want to take with them out into the world. A breathing exercise will be done as reinforcement to the felt sense of spaciousness and internal expansion into healing.

Session Three

The goal of session three is to safely deepen awareness of the fear of losing one's mind and self in addiction, the need to accept "what is" even in the midst of suffering, and to acknowledge the experience of distorted thinking and self-hatred that accompanies addiction's false self. The poems "Cracking Up" and "Who I Am" with writing prompts will be read and discussed. This will then lead into making masks contrasting the addicted false self and the true self. When the masks are completed, the members will be paired so that one member will tell the other the story of his or her mask. This "telling" can take many forms such as talking as in a conversation, by writing a poem, and acting out the spirit of the mask in dance. Each partner will then give feedback on what she or he experienced in this sharing. The group pairs will then share their experience with the entire group. The group session will end with a guided meditation on the chakras ending in the image of the heart chakra and its overflowing compassion.

Session Four

The goal of session four is to gain greater awareness and understanding about shame and co-dependency and what can prompt the wish to be dead. It will be emphasized that suicide is not the answer to a life problem as problems come and go and can be solved, coping strategies can be learned, caring support is available within AA and other resources, but the finality of suicide and its dire consequences on the life lost and those loved ones remaining, lasts forever. Our loved ones grieve endlessly and our own chance at a life of happiness, contribution and recovery is obliterated. Suicide is not the answer. First, session three will be reviewed and what was taken from it briefly shared. The poem "I Am So Sorry" will be read aloud and discussed. The questions accompanying the poem will be read silently and the members will be asked to close their eyes, go within, and feel their inner response to these questions. They will then release this image/feeling into a drawing. Using the ART process (and questions) as developed by Barbara Ganim, they will dialogue with the picture by asking and answering these questions. The members will be given these questions on an accompanying handout with reference cited, for use in this session and future sessions. The image will also be asked "How can I heal from this pain?" The response will be written or drawn and then shared with the group. The group will end with each member saying aloud for whom or what they are grateful.

Session Five

The goal of session five is to openly discuss how violence impacts children from what they witness and what they experience. How these experiences affect the growing child and create risk for addiction will be further explored. As this is a very sensitive subject, group rules for confidentiality and respect for each other will be reiterated. The poem "Questions To A Child" will be read by several group members to hear it in different voices. The beautifully illustrated poem poster may also be shared (please contact Diane Kaufman, MD at artsmedicine@hotmail.com) as the artist Paul Anderson created an oil painting of a mother and child especially for this poem. The poster can also be viewed on the Arts Medicine for Health & Healing website under the My Works section. Possible meanings of the empty heart of the mother in that art work will be discussed. The poem will then be acted out with several members speaking together as the adult voice, several members speaking in response as the child voice, and the rest of the group will be the witness to what is said. Each member still in character as adult, child, and witness will be asked to share his or her feelings about violence and to ask for what he or she needs to be healed. This will first be done in writing and then shared aloud. The session will end with the group members in a circle extending one hand into the center upon which another member will then put his or her hand. Each member will offer a prayer for love and the end of violence, and express what they can and will do to bring peace into the world, as they reach out their hands to each other.

Session Six

The goal of session six is to explore how love can be constructive or destructive in our lives. The group will begin with a review of the prior session. The spoken word video performance of "Desperate Love" will be shown. Next will be reading and discussion of the following poems: "What Is Love," "Now I Know," "How It Feels," and "The Hole In My Heart." From this full discussion of the poem performance and these poems, the group members will create a list of qualities of what love is and what love is not. Each member will be given a paper heart upon which they can write down these qualities and further go on to artistically create and write a True Love Card. Popular love songs and heartbreak songs could be played and sung together. What it means to truly love ourselves will be discussed. The members will then create an "I Love You" card just for themselves. How it feels to focus nurturing and loving energy in our own direction will be discussed. The group will end by singing together, "You have to sing when the spirit says sing." Taking turns they will add their own words such as love, laugh, praise, and more to the song.

Session Seven

The goal of session seven is to explore yearning for forgiveness, the barriers and obstacles we put in its way, and why forgiveness is necessary on the path towards serenity. The previous session will briefly be reviewed. Next, the "letting go" from blame, anger, and guilt into humility, acceptance, and responsibility for self and others will be discussed. The poem "The Place of Forgiveness" will be read aloud. The members will be asked to write on a piece of paper their response to the questions: "For what do you seek forgiveness and from whom? Do you need to forgive another? Do you need to forgive yourself? What is the place of forgiveness in your life?" The role of forgiveness in Alcoholic Anonymous' Step 8 and Step 9 will be discussed. The members will each be given an empty shoe box to symbolize the place of forgiveness. They will use art supplies to draw and collage with words and images from magazines as well as other materials such as stickers, sparkles, feathers, etc., the inner and outer walls and the empty space within to illustrate the place of forgiveness. Their creations will be discussed with the group, and will include how they can take the next step to the place of forgiveness. The members will put their responses to the questions on forgiveness in the inside of their "place of forgiveness" shoe box as the group together recites the 23rd Psalm. The necessity of "walking the talk" will be gently, but firmly reinforced.

Session Eight

The goal of session eight is to name and honor the spiritual self and its "divine spark" within us all. The group members will begin by discussing their experience of session seven and lead into a guided meditation of going inside the vastness of the inner world to the place of forgiveness that is warmed by the light and flame of the spiritual self within. The meditation will include moving the body as the flame is moving inside them. The image, feeling, and message coming from that inner experience of spirit will be poured out on the page, in drawings and words be that poetry, story or stream of consciousness, just as the poem "Poetic Medicine" suggested. The members will be instructed on the art of witnessing in terms of being an open vessel receiving and not judging. They will then pair off and share their experience and drawings with each other as one speaks (gives) and the other witnesses (receives). The responsibility of the one who receives is to respectfully listen and then say back what they have heard in a non-judgmental way. Each member will then write a reflection about this giving and receiving experience. The session will end with the entire group standing together as "divine sparks" within the center of a large circle that is drawn on the floor, and with eyes closed imagining that the circle is growing larger and larger but the flame still is strong. Next the circle grows smaller and smaller until the members enter the flame itself. Participants will share with a partner how it feels to be at the same time one unique person yet also being a valuable part of a larger whole dedicated to a higher purpose.

Session Nine

The goal of session nine is to experience or imagine an inner calling or purpose to one's life. The previous session will be discussed and members will share how well or not well they were able to maintain a connection with their inner "divine spark." The poem "Secret Ambition" will be read aloud. It will then be done as a performance poem by several of the group members to enact and dramatize the self's desire for fulfillment. The group will form a circle and there will be a call and response of each person's name with sound and body movement. The members will then share how this experience felt for them. Next a drawing will be done emerging from being seen with compassionate eyes and beckoned by "one who welcomes you and wants what is best for you." Participants will write about what they imagine their "true calling" truly is, and how they can achieve it. They will reflect upon how attuned they are to their heart's desire. In small groups the members will share with each other their thoughts and feelings evoked by this exercise. The session will end with members naming themselves to the group aloud as their purpose in life: "I am she/he who…" The group as a whole will respond by saying "We welcome you."

Session Ten

The goal of session ten is to examine the process of "letting go" into rebirthing and transforming the self. The group members will first review their experiences in session nine. The poem "A Strange Feeling" will be read aloud and discussed. Transformation will be discussed in terms of dynamic change: to grow is to change is to let go is to grieve is to rejoice at finally growing. The group will divide in two, and dramatize a conversation between caterpillar and butterfly or if they would prefer a tadpole and frog. The purpose of the enactment is to depict the fragmentation, separation, and misunderstanding that we can feel amongst the many lower and higher (against growth and for growth) parts of ourselves. The conversation will end with pairs of caterpillars and butterflies (or tadpoles and frogs) in connection with each other, holding hands, looking into each other's eyes, and sharing with each other with compassion that they are connected to each other, and that growing into the next level is not an abandoning but an allowing of nature to evolve in a most natural way. The group will end with an exercise whereby each member will be given a sheet upon which he/she can draw with magic markers, glue feathers, apply glitter, write words, etc. of their experience of the exercise. They will then perform a dance with another member as witness. The dancers will first cover themselves with the sheet, and then by the end of the dance, will "let go" of the sheet onto the floor as in shedding or casting off the past. The members will then share with each other their thoughts and feelings evoked by the symbolic dance.

Session Eleven

The goal of session eleven is to recognize and inspire the powerful potential for each person to make a difference, and to awaken compassionate joining with other human beings who share this human journey. The group members will first discuss what was meaningful to them from session ten. The poem "The Power of One" will be read aloud and discussed. The group members will be introduced to the mandala as an artistic and spiritual representation of the whole. After a guided meditation, the members will create mandalas representing images and feelings of first powerlessness and then powerfulness. They will transition to making the second mandala following their reflecting upon and then writing responses per Ganim's ART process handout. They will share the meaning of their mandalas with the group. Next the group will be introduced to the concept of the mandorla where "this becomes that" and paradox is resolved. The almond shaped mandorla is the space and shape created from two overlapping circles. The group members will work in pairs to create mandorlas illustrating the paradox and meeting place of "addiction as a curse and addiction as a gift." Again they will share their creation with the group. The poem "Yesterday My Heart Cracked Open" will then be read aloud and discussed in connection with Step 11 and Step 12 of Alcoholic Anonymous. The group members will be led in a guided meditation to the place where the drop of water remains itself even as it merges into the ocean. The group will end with each member standing in a circle reading responsively the poem "I Am This." The members will be instructed to bring to the next session, which concludes the Arts Medicine Transformation Curriculum program, a simple gift symbolic of healing which they will give to another group member. The gift may be homemade or purchased, but if the latter, a dollar limit needs to be set in advance.

Session Twelve

The goal of session twelve is to review and integrate the many experiences of the Arts Medicine Transformation Curriculum program. Group members will discuss what sessions and topics were most meaningful, and which were not helpful at all. Members will share, if they choose to do so, how the program has impacted their own recovery. Suggestions on how to improve the program will be encouraged. The group will discuss and brainstorm how the program can be integrated into their organization's counseling and support services. Potential barriers and obstacles in facilitating the program at their organization will be discussed from both systemic and personal perspectives. The group members will exchange gifts symbolic of healing with each other and explain their special meaning. There will also be strips of colorful paper on which appreciations for each group member can be written and shared aloud. The group members will be asked to complete a survey providing feedback on their experience of the expressive arts program. A resource listing on expressive arts and healing will be provided. Each group member will receive a graduation certificate and with permission, photographs of individuals and the group will be taken. The graduating members as they leave will be given flowers in keeping with the final sentences of *15 Poems to Recovery & Healing*, "God bestows blessings on us all. May we in turn bless ourselves by becoming true to our higher nature. We are all beautiful flowers. Isn't it time we blossomed in the garden?" The session will end with group members standing in a circle holding hands as they share a moment of silence, inner prayers, and gratitude.

Recommended Readings:

Butterworth, E. (2003). *The Creative Life: 7 Keys to Your Inner Genius*. New York: Jeremy P. Tarcher/Putnam.

Ganim, B. (1999). *Art and Healing: Using Expressive Art to Heal Your Body, Mind, and Spirit*. New York: Three Rivers Press.

Johnson, R. A. (1991). *Owning Your Own Shadow: Understanding the Dark Side of the Shadow*. New York: HarperCollins Publishing.

Koestler, A. (1964). *The Act of Creation: A Study of Consciousness and Unconscious in Science and Art*. New York: Dell Publishing Company, Inc.

Orr, G. (2002). *Poetry as Survival*. Athens, Georgia: The University of Georgia Press.

Samuels, M. and Lane, M. R. (1998). *Creative Healing: How to Heal Yourself by Tapping Your Hidden Creativity*. San Francisco: HarperCollins Publishing.

Whitfield, C. (1985). *Alcoholism, Attachments & Spirituality: A Transpersonal Approach*. East Rutherford, New Jersey: Thomas W. Perrin, Inc.

Wilson, B. (1955). *Alcoholics Anonymous: The Story of How Many Thousands of Men and Women Have Recovered from Alcoholism*. New York: Alcoholics Anonymous Publishing, Inc.

The Cracking Up and Back Again: Transformation Through the Expressive Arts workshop curriculum was written in 2008 as the final proposal project for the Salve Regina University (Newport, Rhode Island) Educational Facilitator Certification in the Expressive Arts Institute Program. It was renamed in 2016 as the Arts Medicine Transformation Curriculum.

The poem, "Desperate Love," by Diane Kaufman was written in 1998 and became a spoken word video performance in 2012. The performance artists are Brittaney Ortiz and Ryan G. Clef. The video was directed and edited by Adam McInnis.

The poem, "To All Hearts That Break," was written by Diane Kaufman in 2015 and inspired the song, "I'm Here." The composer and lyricist is Jacqueline Anabwani. The vocalists are Pastor Jennifer DeLosAngeles and Pastor Princess Fils-Aime. The song was produced and arranged at JAMMAN Productions Recording Studios by James Manno. Video production was by Adam McInnis.

For additional information on arts and healing, please see Dr. Kaufman's Arts Medicine for Health and Healing (www.artsmedicineforhealthandhealing.com). Dr. Kaufman is available for presentations, workshops, and consultation, and can be reached at artsmedicine@hotmail.com. Your feedback on your own experience of *15 Poems to Healing & Recovery* and the Arts Medicine Transformation Curriculum workshop series is most welcome!

Made in the USA
San Bernardino, CA
26 March 2017